STAR ★ FILES

LeBron James

Mark Stewart

Chicago, Illinois

Customer Service 888-363-4266
Visit our website at www.raintreelibrary.com

For more information address the publisher:
Raintree, 100 N. LaSalle, Suite 1200, Chicago, IL 60602

Printed and bound in China by South China Printing Company

09 08 07 06
10 9 8 7 6 5 4 3 2 1

Library of Congress Cataloguing in Publication Data
Stewart, Mark.
  LeBron James / Mark Stewart.
      p. cm. -- (Star files)
  Includes bibliographical references and index.
  ISBN 1-4109-1661-8 (library binding - hardcover)
  1. James, LeBron--Juvenile literature. 2. Basketball players--United States--Biography--Juvenile literature. I. Title. II. Series.
  GV884.J36S84 2005
  796.323'.092--dc22

2005005266

Acknowledgments
The publishers would like to thank the following for permission to reproduce photographs:
Corbis pp. **4** (Reuters/Mike Blake), **5** (Marc Serota/Reuters), **7** (Reuters), **8** (Duomo), **13** (l) (Duomo), **12** (Reuters), **14** (Duomo), **17** (Duomo), **18** (r) (Reuters), **19** (Mark Serota/Reuters), **20** (Lucy Nicholson/Reuters), **21** (l) (Reuters), **22** (r) (Reuters), **24** (Hunter Martin), **25** (Reuters), **26** (Mark Serota/Reuters), **27** (Bettmann), **28** (Gary Caskey/Reuters), **30** (Greg Fiume/NewSport), **31** (Hyungwon Kang/Reuters), **33** (Greg Fiume/NewSport), **34** (Aaron Josefczyk/Reuters), **35** (Craig Lassig/Reuters), **36** (l) (Thomas E. Witte/NewSport), **36-37** (Ron Kuntz/Reuters), **38** (Ron Kuntz/Reuters), **42** (l) (Bettmann), **42** (r) (Ron Kuntz/Reuters), **43** (b) (Reuters); Getty Images pp. **4** (Nathaniel S. Butler), **6** (Photodisc), **9** (Photodisc), **10** (Photodisc), **15** (Photodisc), **18** (l); Harcourt Education Ltd pp. **32** (Gareth Boden); Retna p. **23**; Retna Ltd pp. **11** (Gregorio Binuya), **13** (r) (Janette Beckman), **16** (John Spellman), **21** (r) (Rocky Widner), **39** (t), **43** (t) (Gregorio Binuya); Rex Features pp. **22** (l) (Jussi Nukari), **29** (Mirek Towski), **39** (b) (Brian Rasic), **40** (Jussi Nukari), **41** (t & b) (Timo Jaakonaho).
Cover photograph reproduced with permission of Corbis (Hunter Martin).

Quote sources: p. **5** http://news.bbc.co.uk; p. **6** *Student Sports* November 2001; p. **9** http://sportsillustrated.cnn.com; p. **11** http://www.JockBio.com; p. **15** *Bergen Record* July 8, 2002; p. **16** ABC Broadcast January 2003; p. **19** *Sports Illustrated* February 18, 2002; p. **20** http://broward.com; p. **26** *SLAM* May 2004; p. **30** *Beckett Got Sports,* Issue #1 2004; p. **32** *SLAM,* May 2004; pp. **35**, **36**, **39** *Street & Smith s Pro Basketball,* 2004; p. **40** http://sports.espn.go.com.

The publishers would like to thank Rosie Nixon, Charly Rimsa and Marie Lorimer for their assistance in the preparation of this book.

Contents

Any words appearing in the text in bold, **like this**, are explained in the glossary. You can also look out for them in the "Star Words" box at the bottom of each page. **See page 44 for help with basketball terms.**

So Good, So Young

No one in the history of professional basketball has been as good—as young—as LeBron James of the Cleveland Cavaliers. He is not the first player to jump from high school to pro ball, but he is easily the best.

During his first season, LeBron went from shy **rookie** to confident superstar. He excited fans around the country. Before he came along, no one thought a teenager could do so well in the National Basketball Association (NBA). Thanks to LeBron, they had to think again.

ALL ABOUT LEBRON

Born: December 30, 1984
Family: Mother: Gloria James, Children: 1 son (born October 2004)
Height: 6 feet 8 inches (2 meters 3 centimetres)
Weight: 240 pounds (109 kilograms)
Sport: Basketball
Team: Cleveland Cavaliers
Position: Guard/Forward
Favorite athletes: Michael Vick (Atlanta Falcons) and Alex Rodriguez (New York Yankees)
Favorite food: Breakfast cereal

Star Words   idol someone you look up to

Number 23

LeBron has been wearing the number of his basketball **idol**, Michael Jordan, since high school. When Jordan retired, the NBA was worried it would never see a player like him again. Now the "new" number 23 is picking up right where MJ left off.

I'm like a superhero —call me Basketball Man!

Signature style

LeBron is already one of the most recognizable players in sports. His million-dollar smile, his "I-mean-business" game face, and his dramatic windmill dunks have become his **trademarks**.

LeBron is now a star of the Cavaliers.

Find out later

Who is LeBron's favorite musician?

Which other sport did LeBron play in high school?

What is LeBron's favorite car?

rookie someone who has just started doing something. An NBA rookie is a player in his first season.

Hard Times

★ ★ ★ ★ ★ ★ ★ ★ ★ ★ ★ ★

Home turf

The city of Akron is in northern Ohio, an hour south of Cleveland. It is located on a rise (Akron is Greek for "high") above the Cuyahoga River. Akron is a factory city. For years, many of the world's tires and zippers were made there.

LeBron's mother, Gloria James, was very young when LeBron was born. She hoped that her own mother would be able to help her raise her baby. Sadly, LeBron's grandmother was in poor health. She died when LeBron was still a small child. Gloria was left to take care of him alone. It was almost impossible for her to hold down a job and look after LeBron at the same time.

He shoots, he scores

Like most toddlers, LeBron loved to learn and explore. One day, Gloria brought home a small plastic basketball hoop and a tiny rubber ball. LeBron's eyes lit up. He played for hours on end. Every time LeBron put the ball in the basket, a big smile would stretch across his face.

> ❝ My mom and I have always been there for each other. ❞

⭐ Star fact

Today, LeBron's favorite spot in Akron is Swensen's. He says they make the world's best hamburgers.

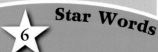

School days

Over the years, Gloria had a hard time paying her rent. She and LeBron had to move many times. LeBron was not happy with this constant change, and it showed in his schoolwork. His elementary-school teachers remember him seeming **distracted**. LeBron did not make many friends as a child because he was embarrassed about his home life.

Father figure

LeBron never knew his father. He **vows** that his own son, born in the fall of 2004, will always have a strong father figure in his life.

Even though LeBron is an NBA star, his mom Gloria is still involved in his life.

vow promise

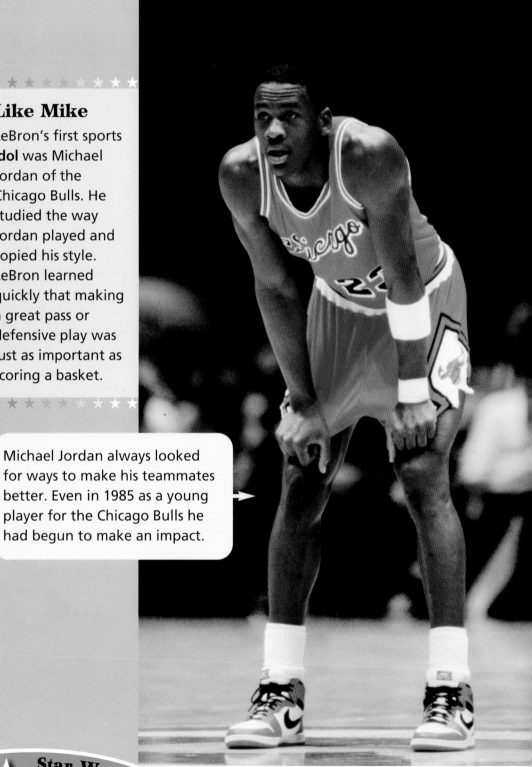

Like Mike

LeBron's first sports **idol** was Michael Jordan of the Chicago Bulls. He studied the way Jordan played and copied his style. LeBron learned quickly that making a great pass or defensive play was just as important as scoring a basket.

Michael Jordan always looked for ways to make his teammates better. Even in 1985 as a young player for the Chicago Bulls he had begun to make an impact.

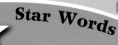

Star Words   secure safe; settled

8

Family matters

According to Gloria James, LeBron's father was named Anthony McClelland. He had no interest in raising children and left before LeBron was born. Gloria's brothers, Terry and Curt, helped out when they could. LeBron looked up to his uncles, who were both good at sports.

Sudden impact

The first man who made a real difference in LeBron's life was Gloria's boyfriend, Eddie Jackson. He helped the family to feel **secure**. LeBron remembers him as an early father figure.

Sports to the rescue

Living in dingy apartments and surrounded by the dangers of the street, LeBron felt "bottled up." He had no way of showing his emotions or creativity. In grade school, LeBron discovered basketball and football. In these games he found the freedom and joy he did not have in the rest of his life.

"You know how a guy can make his team so much better? That's one thing I learned from watching Michael Jordan."

Pee Wee powerhouse

LeBron was a little bigger and a little faster than other children his age. In his first season of Pee Wee football, he scored nineteen touchdowns in six games.

Star student

Living with the Walkers turned LeBron's school life around. As a fifth grader, he won his school's award for perfect attendance.

Big move

Frankie Walker was LeBron's Pee Wee football coach. He saw something special in LeBron and took a real interest in him. When Walker found out that LeBron was skipping school, he offered to let the fourth grader stay with his family. He thought they could offer him the structure and **discipline** he needed. Gloria agreed and for the next 18 months, they lived apart. During this time, LeBron made friends with the Walker's son, Frankie Jr.

Learning more

Walker made sure LeBron went to school and finished his homework. He also taught LeBron more about basketball. Soon, LeBron could shoot, dribble, and pass with both hands.

Like many people, LeBron loved to play basketball with friends.

Star Words

discipline training or encouragement to follow rules and behave well

Gang of six

Every Sunday night, LeBron and Frankie Jr. would play ball at the Akron Jewish Community Center. They formed a team with four other players: Sian Cotton, Willie McGee, Romeo Travis, and Dru Joyce III. LeBron and Dru became best friends.

" The Walkers will never know what a difference they made in my life. "

Coach Keith

LeBron carried on learning about basketball from Keith Dambrot. He was a **volunteer** at the Jewish Community Center where LeBron and Frankie played basketball. Dambrot had been the head basketball coach at Central Michigan University.

★ ★ ★ ★ ★ ★ ★ ★

LeBron is very grateful to the Walkers for all the help they gave him.

volunteer someone who offers to help without being paid

Fab Four

★ ★ ★ ★ ★ ★ ★ ★ ★ ★ ★

Sooooo close

In 1999, the Shooting Stars made it to the AAU eighth grade championship game in Orlando, Florida. LeBron was magnificent against the Southern California All-Stars, but his team was beaten by just a few points.

★ ★ ★ ★ ★ ★ ★ ★ ★ ★ ★

LeBron's basketball skills **blossomed** in sixth grade. Dru, Sian, and Willie also showed they were gifted players. They called themselves the "Fab Four" and were coached by Dru's father, Dru Joyce Jr. That summer, LeBron and his pals formed the heart of the Northeast Ohio Shooting Stars. The Shooting Stars played in lots of **Amateur** Athletic Union (AAU) events. They made it to the championship tournament in Salt Lake City, Utah.

Tall tale

By eighth grade, LeBron and his three basketball buddies had amazing **chemistry** on the court. LeBron stood out as the most talented of the Fab Four. He was also the biggest. By age 14, he stood over 6 feet (1.8 meters) tall.

LeBron and Willie McGee share a joke with other St. V teammates. St. V went on to win this game against Kettering Alter in 2003.

Star Words

amateur   not a professional; not a paid job
blossomed   developed; got much better

LeBron in action for St. V.

Put me in, coach

LeBron looked forward to playing football for St. V. The team's coach was Jay Brophy, a college star for the University of Miami who later played in the National Football League.

Package deal

LeBron, Dru, Willie, and Sian were all offered basketball scholarships by private high schools. They decided it would be fun to go to the same high school together. The thought of landing four-fifths of a varsity basketball team had the city's coaches very excited. The boys chose St. Vincent-St. Mary High School, known by the students as "St. V." St. V was a very good school in downtown Akron. The basketball coach there was Keith Dambrot from their rec-league days.

Derek Jeter of the New York Yankees —a team that LeBron supports.

★ Star fact

LeBron rooted for all of Cleveland's sports teams as a kid, but he secretly liked the Yankees.

Young gun

LeBron played his first high-school basketball game on December 3, 1999 against Cuyahoga Falls. He quickly became the star of St. V's basketball team, known as the Fighting Irish. He led them to a perfect 27–0 record. St. V went on to win the state championship—its first since 1984.

★ ★ ★ ★ ★ ★ ★ ★ ★ ★ ★

Catch me if you can

LeBron was a very good football player. He played for St. V's football team as well as their basketball team. In his second football season, he played wide receiver, gained 700 yards, and was named **All-State**.

★ ★ ★ ★ ★ ★ ★ ★ ★ ★ ★

LeBron was soon the star of the Fighting Irish.

Star Words

All-State honor given to the best high-school players in each state

Like a weed

LeBron grew 4 inches (10 centimeters) the summer after his freshman year and returned to school at 6 feet 7 inches (1.97 meters). The city was buzzing as the season **opener** drew near. There was so much demand for tickets that St. V decided to move the game to the University of Akron. More than 5,000 people filled the James A. Rhodes Arena to watch LeBron.

> I see things on the court before they even happen.

State champions

The Fighting Irish lost just one game during the 2000–2001 season, and won their second state title. The championship game drew more than 17,000 fans. LeBron **dominated** the game and was named Ohio's "Mr. Basketball."

Thousands of fans came to watch the St. V season opener.

dominate control
opener first game

Ready for the pros?

During LeBron's sophomore season, he was matched up against some of the best seniors in the country. Time and again he **dominated** them. This made some people think that at the age of sixteen he might be ready to play pro basketball.

After the season, Michael Jordan and a group of other NBA stars invited LeBron to work out with them. These stars included Antoine Walker and Michael Finley, who also thought LeBron was ready for the pros.

Dear Diary

LeBron is a clear and clever writer. When he was in his junior year, a sports magazine featured some of the things he had written in his basketball diary.

Michael Jordan could see that LeBron was a talented player.

Are you nuts?

LeBron shocked everyone when he decided to play football as a junior instead of resting for the basketball season. He strapped on his helmet and helped a so-so team reach the state championship game. LeBron caught more than 50 passes in 2001 and had a great time, but a broken finger **convinced** him to give up football.

> I believe LeBron James would start on any NBA team today. (Bill Walton, NBA Hall of Famer)

Junior achiever

LeBron ruled the court in 2001–2002. He became the nation's top high-school basketball player. He could handle and shoot the ball as well as a guard, power his way to layups and rebounds like a forward, and defend the basket like a center.

Star Words

convince encourage; help to make up your mind about something

St. V did not win the state championship, but there was little doubt about LeBron's skill. Everyone knew he could skip college basketball and jump straight to the NBA after his senior year.

LeBron was young, but he was ready for the pros.

Hey, I know you

In 2002, Coach Dambrot took a coaching job at the University of Akron. Dru Joyce, Jr.—the father of LeBron's best friend—was hired to coach the Fighting Irish. Joyce had coached LeBron and the Shooting Stars in AAU play.

Eye of the Storm

LeBron's senior year at St. V was like a roller-coaster ride. It had its ups and downs, but it was fun all the way. LeBron's game continued to improve. He also found many ways to make his teammates better. Romeo, Dru, and Sian played well enough to earn college **scholarships**.

★ ★ ★ ★ ★ ★ ★ ★ ★ ★

Book smart

LeBron finished school with a solid grade-point average, and could have gone to any college in the country. His best subject was Earth Science.

★ ★ ★ ★ ★ ★ ★ ★ ★ ★

LeBron's fans could watch him play on television.

Star Words   controversy scandal

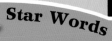

In the state championship game, LeBron took over in the fourth quarter to help St. V win the title.

> At this age, LeBron is better than anybody I've ever seen. (Sonny Vaccaro, Footwear Executive)

Don't touch that dial

LeBron's fame produced millions of dollars during his senior year. Most of that money went to his school, which sold the television rights to its games. Some of his games ended up as pay-per-view events—the first time high-school basketball had been sold in this way.

Hot water

LeBron was at the center of two **controversies** during his senior year. The first was when Gloria took out a $50,000 loan to buy a new car. Some people thought that she was wrongly benefiting from her son's stardom. A month later, LeBron was **suspended** for accepting a gift of two retro jerseys from a sports shop. There are strict rules against **amateur** athletes making money from their fame and it took a judge to overturn this ruling.

★ Star fact

LeBron averaged 31.6 points, 9.6 rebounds, and 4.6 assists as a senior, and was named National Player of the Year for the second year in a row. In 4 years of high-school ball he totaled 2,657 points, 892 rebounds, and 523 assists.

Sole man

LeBron was the grand prize in a fierce **bidding war** between the world's top sneaker companies. Everyone wanted LeBron to wear their shoes. It was Nike who won in the end. LeBron wore the sneakers modeled on his favorite car—the Hummer—on court for Cleveland.

LeBron in his Nike sneakers.

Nod of approval

One of LeBron's proudest moments in high school was the day he heard that there would be a Lebron James bobble-head doll.

LeBron at an All-Star contest in 2003.

Teen dreams

After winning the 2003 state championship, LeBron appeared in two "showcase" tournaments for high-school seniors. Many of the players were **auditioning** for college scholarships. LeBron was just there to have fun. Although he had not announced it yet, everyone knew he was headed directly to the NBA.

It's official

As expected, LeBron held a press conference to tell the world he would enter the NBA Draft. There was a good chance he would end up playing near his hometown, for the Cleveland Cavaliers. This made the day even more exciting for LeBron.

> I'm one of the most highly **publicized** players in the country right now and I haven't even played one game of basketball in the NBA.

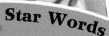

Star Words   audition chance for an athlete to show his or her skills

Holy Moses!

The first high-school player to make a successful jump to the pros was Moses Malone. He joined the Utah Stars in 1974 and went on to have a Hall of Fame career.

Kobe Bryant was another high-school success to make it straight to the NBA.

LeBron told the world at this press conference that he was entering the NBA Draft.

Those who came before me

LeBron was not the first high-school player to jump directly to the pros. There have been a few others, including current stars Kobe Bryant and Kevin Garnett. Some make it, and some do not. A player who fails cannot go back and play in college, meaning that he is gambling with his education.

Luck of the draw

The Cleveland Cavaliers lost 65 games out of 82 in 2002–2003. This meant they had the best chance of winning the first pick in the NBA Draft. Nevertheless, Cleveland fans were holding their breath until the **outcome** was clear. The team with the most losses does not always get the first pick. Luckily for the "Cavs," the odds worked in their favor this time and they were awarded the number-one selection. They chose LeBron.

LeBron was happy to be chosen by the Cavs.

We're number one!

LeBron joined a **select** group when he was chosen first in the Draft. Other number ones include all-time greats Tim Duncan, Allen Iverson (above), Shaquille O'Neal, David Robinson, Hakeem Olajuwon, Magic Johnson, Bill Walton, Kareem Abdul-Jabbar, Oscar Robertson, Wilt Chamberlain, and Elgin Baylor.

Star Words

debate discussion or argument
outcome result

A new era

LeBron's team had joined the NBA in 1970. In all the years that followed, the Cavs had only a handful of winning seasons, and they had never come close to winning a championship. The pressure was on LeBron to help turn the team around.

Bold predictions

Pro scouts had seen LeBron play, but only against other high-school teams. They were divided on how he would do against **seasoned** pros. Some said he would be **overwhelmed** by NBA competition and wind up on the bench. Others said he was already better than half the players in the league. The **debate** went on all summer.

David Stern is the commissioner of the NBA and oversees the Draft.

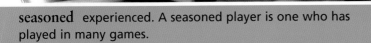

seasoned experienced. A seasoned player is one who has played in many games.

Summer of love

Cleveland is one of the United States' biggest sports towns. The city has been host to professional baseball since the 1870s. Three different pro football teams have done well there. Basketball is another story. The Cavaliers never caused much excitement in Cleveland. The team had never challenged for a championship. They had never had a true superstar until LeBron.

Money!

The NBA puts a limit on the amount of money a team can pay its players. There is no limit, however, to what a player can make from **endorsing** products. LeBron's **rookie** salary made him a millionaire. This was nothing, though, compared to what he will receive from the shoe, soda, candy, trading card, and sports drink products he endorses.

LeBron at the launch of the Air Zoom Generation sneakers.

Star Words

endorse when a famous person is paid for wearing, appearing on, or using a certain product

Paul Silas was LeBron's first NBA coach.

Paul Silas

LeBron's first NBA coach, Paul Silas, was an ideal guide for the young star. Silas had been a good **role-player** and a member of several championship teams. He also had a "fatherly" side that LeBron loved.

Learning the drill

LeBron's greatest challenge as an NBA rookie was getting used to the speed and power of the pro game. He also had to learn the different plays used by the Cavalier offense. LeBron worked hard in training camp and got ready for the long, 82-game season ahead.

role-player player who concentrates on just one area of his game, for example defense, rebounding, or outside shooting

Rookie Treatment

Young stars

The team LeBron joined became a lot better than most NBA fans thought. Young, enthusiastic players such as Ricky Davis, Carlos Boozer, Dajuan Wagner, and Darius Miles made the Cavs a dangerous team.

In the NBA, it does not matter how famous a **rookie** is. He still gets the "rookie treatment" from his teammates. It is a **rite of passage**. The team played a good joke on LeBron and Jason Kapono at the beginning of an **exhibition game**. They told them to lead the team on to the court when the Cavs were announced. Then they stayed behind while the two rookies sprinted on to the court alone!

> If I just kept doing what I was doing in high school, nothing was going to change.

Darius Miles and Ricky Davis were two of LeBron's Cavs teammates.

Star Words

exhibition game non-league game that is practice for the players and entertainment for the fans

The day before his NBA debut, LeBron had lunch with Hall of Famer Moses Malone. Malone (right) was the first player to make a successful move from high school to the pros.

Starting lineup

LeBron made the starting lineup for Cleveland's season **opener**. He played alongside Ricky Davis, Darius Miles, Carlos Boozer, and Zydrunas Ilgauskas. LeBron was nervous in his NBA **debut** against the Sacramento Kings on October 29, 2003. He made some mistakes, but also scored 25 points and had 9 assists and 4 steals. Cleveland lost, but the team had clearly improved.

Above the rim

The legend of LeBron James began for real in a December practice. A bad "alley-oop" pass from a teammate soared over his head as he angled toward the basket. LeBron rose off the floor and snatched the ball with one hand. He was so far off the ground that his chest was at rim level. LeBron then took the ball and threw it down through the basket—he was too high in the air to dunk!

Aiming high

At eighteen, LeBron was not expected to challenge any league records for rookies. That did not mean they were out of reach, though. Oscar Robertson held the record for points in a season by a rookie guard (2,165), while Earl Monroe held the single-game scoring record for rookie guards (56).

rite of passage something that happens when you move from one stage of life to another

Under the radar

Fans overlooked three other great rookies from 2003–2004. Chris Bosh of the Toronto Raptors, Dwyane Wade of the Miami Heat, and Kirk Hinrich of the Chicago Bulls all had amazing years, too.

Carmelo and me

The player that LeBron was compared to most during his **rookie** year was Carmelo Anthony of the Denver Nuggets. Carmelo was a year older than LeBron. He had played one season of college basketball before entering the NBA. He led his college, Syracuse University, to the national championship. Many experts believed this experience would give Carmelo the edge over LeBron during the 2003–2004 NBA season.

LeBron was often compared to Carmelo Anthony.

media event something that gets the attention of newspapers, magazines, television, and radio shows

One-on-one

The first meeting between LeBron and Carmelo was a big **media event**. Around 300 reporters covered the game, which was televised around the country. LeBron only scored seven points, but he had eleven rebounds and seven assists. Fans were disappointed that the two young stars only guarded each other for a few minutes. The Nuggets won the game, 93–89.

Better by the minute

With LeBron getting better each game, the Cavaliers got better as a team. They began winning games they used to lose, and earned the respect of the league. LeBron's drives to the basket gave his teammates a chance to shine, too. Carlos Boozer, for example, **blossomed** into a star.

Carmelo Anthony played for Syracuse in college.

Beyond compare

Although he was still a teenager, LeBron found himself being compared to some of the best players in the league. LeBron was **versatile** enough to play every position except center, and was a threat to score twenty points or more on any given night.

Star crossed

Despite lots of support from his hometown fans, LeBron was not voted on to the starting Eastern Conference All-Star team. When he was not chosen as a reserve, people thought the NBA had kept its most exciting young player out of the All-Star spotlight. LeBron did play in the **Rookie** Challenge Game during All-Star Weekend. He scored 33 points.

Report card

Pro scouts gave LeBron an "A" for the first half of his rookie season. The skills that made him a great high-school player got better and better in the NBA.

> He's so fast it's scary. (Dirk Nowitzki, Dallas Mavericks All-Star)

Dirk Nowitzki has played against some great players, such as Michael Jordan— shown here playing for the Washington Wizards.

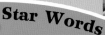

Star Words   acquired buy or become the owner of something

Opposition players worked hard to try and stop LeBron driving forward.

Once LeBron became comfortable in the NBA, teams had to think up ways to stop him. On offense, they decided to give him long, open shots. On defense, they saw that he was unsure of how to fight his way through picks and screens. Until LeBron improved in these areas, this would be the way to beat him.

What's the point?

A January trade of Ricky Davis left a hole at the point guard position for the Cavs. The team had just **acquired** Jeff McInnis, but he was injured and could not play. Until Jeff was ready to play again, LeBron was made the Cav's floor leader. He did a great job, and earned a lot of respect from his teammates.

Method man

LeBron spent the second half of his rookie year playing beside new point guard Jeff McInnis. He watched how clever McInnis was on the court. LeBron learned a lot of tricks to use in his own game.

versatile good at lots of different things

On the Road Again

★ ★ ★ ★ ★ ★ ★ ★ ★ ★ ★

Fan favorites

Thanks to LeBron, the Cavs had sixteen of their games televised nationally in 2003–2004. This was more than in the last 10 years put together! Cleveland finished the year with sixteen sellouts.

★ ★ ★ ★ ★ ★ ★ ★ ★ ★

LeBron eats a lot of cereal. It is his favorite food!

The second half of LeBron's first NBA season challenged him like never before. In high school, he had played around 30 games a year. In the NBA, there are 82 games a year. There was also the pressure of the playoff hunt. The Cavs had a chance to advance to post-season for the first time in years.

Where am I?

The life of an NBA star is not as glamorous as fans might think. LeBron was mobbed wherever he went. He was too young to go to nightclubs, so he could not hang out with his older teammates. Basically, he played a lot of video games and ate a lot of cereal. When the Cavs were on the road, LeBron would sometimes wake up and have no idea where he was.

> In the beginning I was holding back, trying to feel my spot, trying to feel what the team wanted me to do.

⭐ Star fact

In 2004–2005 a record 30 Cavs games were aired nationally on television.

Star Words home stretch last part of something; nearly finished

Shouldering the load

After a good start, the Cavs began to lose more often than they won. LeBron was able to keep up his level of play, but still felt responsible for the team's problems. When his teammates saw this, they realized he was a true team player.

Go-to guy

As the Cavaliers struggled down the **home stretch**, they looked to LeBron for help. When they needed a basket, they wanted the ball in his hands. Though still a teenager, LeBron had become the team's leader.

Life on the road can be very tiring.

In the final weeks of the season, LeBron's outside shooting improved so much that teams had to guard him far from the basket. He caused the opposition defenses a lot of headaches!

Most NBA **rookies** "hit the wall" after around 50 games. They lose the spring in their legs and their arms begin to feel heavy. LeBron was the exception to this rule. His muscular **physique** helped him survive the pounding he took on the court. His legs actually got fresher in the final months. Instead of losing a step to defenders, he gained a step on them.

In this game, LeBron flew from just inside the foul line for a fourth quarter dunk!

Star Words

enforcers strong, powerful players
intimidate threaten or scare

LeBron's strong body helped to keep his game at a top level.

Screen test

LeBron had been learning how to create open shots by using screens. This meant that his teammates would get in the way of the defenders, giving him room to get free. He also got better at fighting through screens on defense. This showed how quickly LeBron was learning the pro game.

> It was amazing to me how quickly he picked up the **nuances** of the game.
> (Paul Silas, Cleveland coach)

Playing rough

LeBron's energy frustrated many opponents. The league's "enforcers" tried to **intimidate** him by pushing him around. At a rock-hard 240 pounds (109 kilograms), however, LeBron could take care of himself.

Double trouble

The most difficult adjustment for LeBron was dealing with double-teams—when he was being guarded by two players. He did not always make the right decision when this happened.

nuances slight changes or differences
physique form and size of a person's body

35

Don't forget Dajuan!

Don't forget Dajuan!

Almost forgotten during LeBron's marvelous rookie season was backup guard Dajuan Wagner (below). Just a year older than LeBron, Wagner was expected to become the team's star shooting guard.

So close

With ten games to go, the Cavs were closing in on a playoff spot. Seven straight losses ruined their chances, and the team fell short by one win. LeBron played well, but the team was tired out and lost many opportunities.

> He's special because he lived up to **unprecedented hype**
> (Rick Mahorn, Former NBA Star)

One-man show

LeBron did it all when the season was on the line. He left no doubt that he was for real. LeBron's performances made him only the third **rookie** in history to average twenty points, five rebounds, and five assists. The other two rookies were Oscar Robertson and Michael Jordan.

Star Words

hype building up of something or someone by newspapers, magazines, television, and radio shows

On the rebound

Despite falling short of the playoffs, the Cavs showed improvement where it counts. They increased their number of wins from 17 to 35. They also showed their **persistence** by leading the NBA in team rebounds.

LeBron enjoyed his basketball right up to the end of the season. Here, he goes to the hoop in a game where he scored seventeen points.

Strengths and weaknesses

As a rookie, LeBron was at his best in the open court. Once LeBron got going there was no stopping him. LeBron's weakest area was his choice of shot. He often settled for long shots instead of working for better, closer ones.

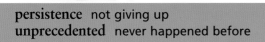
persistence not giving up
unprecedented never happened before

37

Just Rewards

LeBron finished his first NBA season averaging 20.9 points per game. He also became the youngest player in history to score 1,000 points. His best game was against the New Jersey Nets during the heat of the playoff race. He scored 41 points and dished out 13 assists. These numbers were good enough to earn LeBron the **Rookie** of the Year award. He beat Carmelo Anthony in a close vote. LeBron also finished among the NBA's Top 10 in the Most Valuable Player voting.

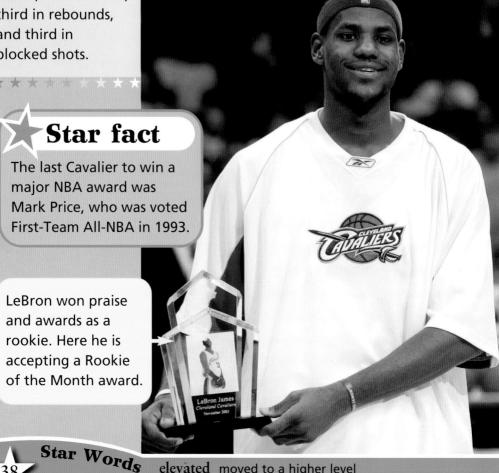

★ Star fact

The last Cavalier to win a major NBA award was Mark Price, who was voted First-Team All-NBA in 1993.

LeBron won praise and awards as a rookie. Here he is accepting a Rookie of the Month award.

Star Words elevated moved to a higher level

LeBron now needs security staff with him when he travels.

Fatherhood

Now that LeBron is a proud father, his biggest challenge off the court will be finding the right balance between being a kid and raising a kid.

Thanks, Mom

LeBron and his mom are still a team. She nearly always goes to watch him play and is always there for him whenever he needs her.

"His whole game [the way he played] just **elevated**. (Paul Silas, Cavs coach)"

Thanks to LeBron, after years of struggle Gloria James is finally living the good life.

Kicking back

LeBron knows how to relax and have fun like any teenager. He still hangs out with his friends and family. He still plays video games and listens to Jay-Z for hours a day. LeBron still plays the playground shooting game H-O-R-S-E with those crazy enough to challenge him.

Jay-Z is LeBron's favorite musician.

Olympic shock

The U.S. Olympic team was surprised by defeats against Puerto Rico, Lithuania, and Argentina, and had to settle for a bronze medal. Many wondered why LeBron did not play more.

All that glitters

When USA Basketball was getting together its team for the 2004 Olympics, many NBA stars refused to go because of security concerns. When LeBron was invited to play, he jumped at the chance. He wanted to add a gold medal to his trophy case.

You're late!

LeBron thought the Olympics were all fun and games. He was wrong. LeBron was benched by coach Larry Brown—along with Allen Iverson and Amare Stoudemire—for being late to a team meeting.

> " I feel like I'm going to be able to control my own destiny. "

Carmelo (left) and LeBron hardly got to play for Team USA.

Star Words   destiny future

Riding the pine

One of the major reasons why LeBron agreed to join the Olympic squad was the chance to play for Larry Brown. The **legendary** coach had just won the NBA championship. Although he learned a lot in practice, LeBron and fellow **rookie** Carmelo Anthony barely got to play.

Larry Brown is a famous coach and LeBron could not wait to work with him.

LeBron used the Olympics as a learning experience.

Sound advice

LeBron used his time at the Olympics to learn from his more experienced teammates. They gave him an idea of the challenges that were ahead.

legendary   very well-known and well-respected

Having a Ball

LeBron's basketball life is just beginning, but he already knows about the adventures, opportunities, and challenges that await him in the NBA. He knows he is "the man" and he is comfortable in that role. LeBron has always found ways to make his teammates better, and this is his goal in the coming years. If he improves as much as most people expect, Cleveland may have a shot at its first NBA championship banner.

Building block

LeBron is the centerpiece of a **rebuilding program** by general manager Jim Paxson and coach Paul Silas. Paxson was a teammate of superstar Clyde Drexter on the exciting Portland teams of the 1980s.

Home games

LeBron is the first person in a long time to be an NBA star in his own city. The last player to do this was Wilt Chamberlain (above). He scored big in his hometown of Philadelphia more than 40 years ago.

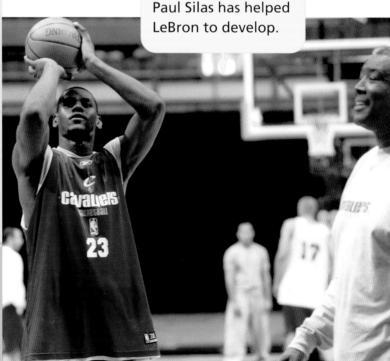

Paul Silas has helped LeBron to develop.

Star Words   memorabilia things that remind you of a famous person or place

Silas played alongside John Havlicek and Dave Cowens on championship teams in Boston. Both clubs specialized in surrounding superstars with smart **role-players,** which is what the Cavs must do with LeBron.

How good? How great!

The sky is the limit for LeBron James. He combines great physical talent, intelligence, and instincts—with an enthusiasm for life and basketball that excites everyone who comes into contact with him. Will LeBron be the best ever? Only time will tell. Will he change the game? He already has!

LeBron has a huge following of fans hoping for autographs, or photos of him.

★ Star fact

LeBron's favorite car is the Hummer. He bought one soon after he entered the NBA.

The shirt off his back

LeBron's number 23 jersey is the top seller among NBA fans. Cleveland Cavalier **memorabilia** skyrocketed to number five in sales during the 2003–2004 season.

rebuilding program organized effort to make things better

Basketball 101

Common terms

alley-oop	pass thrown to a player who has already started rising to the basket
dribble	bouncing the ball
dunk	shot that is slammed into the basket with one or two hands
fade-away	trying to shoot while jumping away from the basket
hook	sweeping shot taken with the body between the defender and the ball
jump shot	shot released as a player rises in the air
lane	large, rectangular area in front of the basket
layup	short shot released while moving toward the basket
pick	obstruction made by a player to "pick off" a teammate's defender
screen	obstruction made by a player to help a teammate get free or open

Violations

double dribble	when a player stops his dribble, then starts it again
foul	illegal contact between players on different teams
goaltending	when a player touches a ball that is directly above the basket, or on its way down toward the basket
traveling	when a player with the ball takes too many steps without dribbling

Statistics

assist	pass that leads to a basket
blocked shot	shot that is deflected or batted away

free throw	unobstructed shot given to a player after he has been fouled
rebound	controlling the ball after a missed shot
steal	ball that is intercepted or taken from a player on the opposite team
three-pointer	long shot from behind the three-point line
turnover	play that results in loss of possession of the ball

Positions

center	player tall enough to rebound and score close to the basket, or to be the last line of defense against layups, dunks, and other short shots
forward	player big enough to play close to the basket; a "power forward" is asked to score inside and collect rebounds, while a "small forward" must play in a larger area
guard	player who handles the ball most often; a "point guard" does most of the dribbling, while a "shooting guard" is expected to score

Find Out More

Books

Jones, Ryan. *King James: Believe the Hype: The LeBron James Story*. New York: St. Martin's Griffin, 2003.

Morgan Jr., David Lee. *LeBron James: The Rise of a Star*. Cleveland: Gray & Company Publishers, 2003.

Glossary

acquired buy or become the owner of something

All-State honor given to the best high-school players in each state

amateur not a professional; not a paid job

audition chance for an athlete to show his or her skills

bidding war when people or companies compete for something. The side that offers the most money usually wins.

blossomed developed; got much better

chemistry working really well together

controversy scandal

convince encourage; help to make up your mind about something

debate discussion or argument

debut first

destiny future

discipline training or encouragement to follow rules and behave well

distracted not able to concentrate

dominate control

elevated moved to a higher level

endorse when a famous person is paid for wearing, appearing on, or using a certain product

enforcers strong, powerful players

exhibition game non-league game that is practice for the players and entertainment for the fans

home stretch last part of something; nearly finished

hype building up of something or someone by newspapers, magazines, television, and radio shows

idol someone you look up to

intimidate threaten or scare

investment putting money into something, hoping to get more money back

legendary very well-known and well-respected

media event something that gets the attention of newspapers, magazines, television, and radio shows

memorabilia things that remind you of a famous person or place

nuances slight changes or differences

opener first game

outcome result

overwhelmed unable to cope

persistence not giving up

physique form and size of a person's body

publicized written about in magazines and newspapers

rebuilding program organized effort to make things better

rite of passage something that happens when you move from one stage of life to another

role-player player who concentrates on just one area of his game, for example defense, rebounding, or outside shooting

rookie someone who has just started doing something. An NBA rookie is a player in his first season.

scholarship when a student is given money to help them go to a school or college

seasoned experienced. A seasoned player is one who has played in many games.

secure safe; settled

select small group, carefully chosen

suspended stopped or banned from playing for a period of time

trademark certain thing that is connected with a certain person

unprecedented never happened before

versatile good at lots of different things

volunteer someone who offers to help without being paid

vow promise

Index